*Leader's Guide for
the group study of*

BE MATURE

By Warren W. Wiersbe

Leader's Guide prepared by
FAITH MARKLE

Instructions and 12 Multiuse Transparency Masters (for visual aids) are included in a removable center section. Unless otherwise noted, Scripture quotations are from the King James Version. Other quotations are from *The New American Standard Bible* (NASB), © 1960, 1962, 1963, 1968, 1971, 1972, 1973 by the Lockman Foundation, La Habra, California. Used by permission.

VICTOR BOOKS

a division of SP Publications, Inc., Wheaton, Illinois
Offices also in Fullerton, California • Whitby, Ontario, Canada • London, England

ISBN: 0-88207-985-9

Suggested Teaching Methods

Brainstorming. Announce the question or topic to be "stormed." Members make as many informal suggestions as possible, not waiting to be called on. No criticism of suggestions is allowed. List suggestions on board; when all are in, have class evaluate and discuss the ideas. This method loosens up the group, involves nonparticipants, and produces new ideas.

Buzz Groups. Divide the class into groups, with from three to six persons, depending on size of class, in a group. Appoint a leader for each group or let groups select own leaders. Assign a topic to each group. Several—or all—groups can discuss same topic if necessary. Allow 5-8 minutes for discussion in the groups, then reconvene entire class and get reports from group leaders. Jot findings on board for discussion by entire class. Many persons are freer to express themselves in small groups, so this method provides maximum participation and interaction.

Discussion. Not to be confused with *Question and Answer.* In discussion, members react not only with the teacher but with one another. Usually discussion is started by the teacher's asking a question to which there is more than a single acceptable answer. ("Where was the Sea of Galilee?" is hardly a discussion question!) A student will respond to a question, someone else may disagree with him, and a third person may have additional comments. The teacher is responsible for starting the discussion, keeping it "on track" by asking leading questions as necessary, and summarizing it after contributions cease. If a discussion gets out of hand and rambles, much of its value is lost.

Group (or Class) Bible Study. Each person should have his Bible open. Ask questions that will help the class learn what the passage you are studying says. Encourage sharing of insights as group discusses the interpretation of the passage and its application to current needs. Always summarize findings. This method makes students think; it shows them how to study the Bible on their own; and it increases participation and involvement.

Interview. Ask questions—or have someone in the class ask questions—of the person being interviewed. He will ordinarily be a "resource" person—one who has a fund of specialized knowledge on which you will draw. Or, an interview can be a variation on *Role Play* (see page 4).

Lecture. Needs no definition! If you lecture, aim to be *interesting* —well-prepared, enthusiastic, cordial, relevant, and with perhaps a touch of humor when it is in good taste.

Listening Groups. Same as *Buzz Groups,* except that each group is assigned a topic to listen for as someone reads a selection—Scripture or something else—or discusses a subject. When the class is reassembled as a whole, group leaders report and then the entire class evaluates the reports.

Neighbor Nudging. Like *Buzz Groups,* except that there are only two people, sitting next to each other, in each "group." In couples' classes the neighbors can be man-and-wife teams, or you may want to have the men on one set of teams and the women on another. (If a person is left out in the pairing off, assign him to one of the twosomes.) This method makes it easy for bashful persons to participate. However, since there are no group leaders, it may be hard to get some "neighbors" to speak up in the general session following the nudging.

Question and Answer. Teacher asks questions and students answer them. Makes for good interaction between teacher and students. Teacher should word questions carefully in advance—imprecise, confusing questions will be the death of this method, which provides involvement, guides group thinking, and keeps the class on the assigned topic, preventing "wandering."

Reading Groups. Same as *Buzz Groups* or *Listening Groups*, except that members of the group are assigned a passage of Scripture (or something else) to read and are given questions to be answered on the basis of the selection. The entire class then discusses the reports of the groups. In *Reading Groups* there are ordinarily no leaders, though in larger groups they may be helpful.

Skit. Have members read the parts of a brief script that highlights a point, provokes discussion, or presents information. Provides good variety.

Role Play. Two (or more) class members, without advance notice or written scripts, act out a situation or relationship. Give them directions as to the kind of people they are to represent and the situation in which they find themselves. They speak extemporaneously. Follow with analysis and evaluation by the class. This method helps people "feel" situations, gives them opportunity to try different solutions, and creates interest at the beginning of class. Helps apply Scripture to interpersonal relationships.

Study Groups. Like *Buzz Groups*, but instead of discussing a subject, the groups study a passage, examining it for what it says, what it means, or how it may best be applied. Each group has a leader.

Discussion is by far the best single method. If your group participates well in discussion, you will have little need for the other methods—which, after all, are designed primarily to stimulate discussion. If your class sits glumly silent instead of getting into a discussion, use other methods indicated to loosen them up.

Here are a few rules for leading discussion:
1. Maintain a relaxed, informal atmosphere.
2. Don't call on people by name to participate unless you are quite sure they are willing to do so.
3. Give a person lots of time to answer a question. If necessary, restate the question casually and informally.
4. Acknowledge any contribution, regardless of its merit.
5. Don't correct or otherwise embarrass a person who gives a wrong answer. Thank him; then ask the class, "What do the rest of you think?" or, "Has someone else another view?"
6. If some individual monopolizes the discussion, say, "On the next question, let's hear from someone who hasn't spoken yet." If necessary, ask the "monopolizer" privately, after class, to give other people more time to answer questions.
7. If someone goes off on a tangent, wait for him to draw a breath; then say, "Thanks for those interesting comments, Joe. Now let's get back to . . ." and mention the subject under consideration, or ask or restate a question that will bring the discussion back on target.
8. If someone asks a question, allow others in the group to give their answers before you give yours.

General Preparation

Survey the entire *Text* and this *Leader's Guide*. *This is basic*. Underline important passages in the text and make notes as ideas come to you, before you forget them. Become familiar with the entire course, including all units in the *Guide* that you will be using in your study. A general knowledge of what is coming up later will enable you to conduct each session more effectively and to keep discussion relevant to the subject at hand. If questions are asked that will be considered later in the course, postpone discussion until that time.

Add to your teaching notes any material and ideas you think important or of special help to your class. As teacher, your enthusiasm for the subject and your personal interest in those you teach, will in large measure determine the interest and response of your class.

We recommend strongly that you plan to use teaching aids, even if you merely jot down a word or two on a chalkboard from time to time to impress a point on the class. When you ask for a number of answers to a question, as in brainstorming, always jot down each answer in capsule form, to keep all ideas before the group. If no chalkboard is available, use a magic marker on large sheets of newsprint over a suitable easel. A printer can supply such paper for you at modest cost.

Once you have decided what visual or audio aids you will use, make sure *all* the necessary equipment is on hand *before* classtime. If you use electrical equipment such as projector or recorder, make sure you have an extension cord available if needed. For chalkboards, have chalk and eraser. That's obvious, of course, but small details are easily forgotten.

Encourage class members to bring Bibles or New Testaments to class and use them. It is good to have several modern-speech translations on hand for purposes of comparison.

Getting Started Right

Start on time. This is especially important for the first session for two reasons. First, it will set the pattern for the rest of the course. If you begin the first lesson late, members will have less reason for being on time at the others. Those who are punctual will be robbed of time, and those who are habitually late will come still later next time. Second, the first session should begin promptly because getting acquainted, explaining the procedure, and introducing the textbook will shorten your study time as it is.

Begin with prayer, asking the Holy Spirit to open hearts and minds, to give understanding, and to apply the truths that are studied. The Holy Spirit is the great Teacher. No teaching, however orthodox and carefully presented, can be truly Christian or spiritual without His control.

Involve everyone. The suggested plans for each session provide a maximum of participation for members of your class. This is important because—

1. People are usually more interested if they take part.
2. People remember more of what they discuss together than they

do of what they are told by a lecturer.
  3. People like to help arrive at conclusions and applications. They are more likely to act on truth if they apply it to themselves than if it is applied to them by someone else.

To promote relaxed involvement, you may find it wise to—
  1. Have the class sit in a circle or semicircle. Some who are not used to this idea may feel uncomfortable at first, but the arrangement makes class members feel more at home. It will also make discussion easier and more relaxed.
  2. Remain seated while you teach (unless the class numbers over 25).
  3. Be relaxed in your own attitude and manner. Remember that the class is not "yours," but the Lord's, so don't get tense!
  4. Use some means to get the class better acquainted, unless all are well known to each other. At the first meeting or two each member could wear a large-lettered name tag. Each one might also briefly tell something about himself, and perhaps tell what, specifically, he expects to get from this study.

Adapting the Course

This material is designed for quarterly use on a weekly basis, but it may be readily adapted to different uses. Those who wish to teach the course over a 12 or 13 week period may simply follow the lesson arrangement as it is given in this *Guide,* using or excluding review/examination sessions as desired.

For 10 sessions, the class may combine four of the shorter lessons into two. The same procedure should be followed for five sessions. However, if the material is to be covered in five sessions, each one should be two hours long with a 10-minute break near the middle. Divide the text chapters among the sessions as needed.

An Alternate Approach

The lesson plans outlined for each session in this *Guide* assume that class members are reading their texts before each class meets. The teacher should make every effort to spark interest in the text by giving members provocative assignments (as suggested under each session) and by such methods as reading aloud an especially fascinating passage (very brief) from the next week's text.

When for any reason, most of the class members will *not* have read the text in advance, (as when the class meets each evening in Vacation Bible School and members work during the day, or as in the first session, when texts may not have been available previously), a slightly different procedure must be followed.

At the beginning of the period, divide the class into small study groups of from four to six persons. Don't separate couples. It is not necessary for the same individuals to be grouped together each time the class meets—though if members prefer this, by all means allow them to meet together regularly.

As teacher of the class, lead one of the study groups yourself. Appoint a leader for each of the other groups. If people are reluctant to be leaders, explain that they need not teach and that they need no advance knowledge of the subject.

Allow the groups and their leaders as much as half an hour to study the textbook together. Then reassemble the class. Ask leaders to report findings or questions of unusual interest or that provoked disagreement. Ask the class the questions you want discussed, and allow questions from your students. Be sure to summarize, in closing, what has been studied. Finally, urge each member of the class to make some specific application of the lesson to his life. Use any of the material in this *Guide* that is appropriate and for which you have time.

Time to Grow Up / *Text, Chapter 1*

Session Goals

1. To become familiar with the historical background of the Book of James.

2. To gain an overview of the content and theme of the book.

3. To learn how to approach this study of James to gain the greatest possible benefit.

Preparation

Distribute the texts to the members of your group a week or two prior to your first session, informing them that *Be Mature* is a study of the Book of James. Ask them to read or skim the five chapters of James, preferably in one sitting, as well as chapter 1 of the text in preparation for the first group session.

Read the entire Book of James several times in various translations, and at least once in one sitting. Reread chapter 1 of the text, outlining or underlining key ideas as you read. Keep in mind the goals of the session as you familiarize yourself with the lesson material. Prepare chalkboard 1.

For your own enrichment, you may wish to read background articles on the Book of James from Bible commentaries, dictionaries, or handbooks you have available to you.

Presentation

1. To begin the session, ask the group, "As you browse through the bookshelves at your favorite bookstore or library, what do you notice about a particular book to determine whether or not you want to read it?" Write their responses on the chalkboard in a column, leaving some space between each word. Comment as follows: "Often you really *can* tell a lot about a book by its cover. If the Book of James were to be reprinted today to take its place next to the many books on the market, we could probably get a good idea of what the book was about by looking at its cover and introductory pages. Let's imagine what we'd find on those pages."

Ask the group to answer each of the following questions, based on their reading from the text. As responses are given, write them on the chalkboard (see chalkboard 1). Add any heading you need as you come to it in the discussion outlined below.

Title. Write on the chalkboard "The Epistle of James" and comment that while this title does not contain a wealth of information, we do know the book is a letter written by a James somebody to someone. Then ask the group, *What subtitle would you give to the book?* (For example, Marks of a Mature Christian, Handbook on Mature Christian Living.)

Author. Ask, *Who is the author of the book?* If "James" is the response, ask further, *How would you distinguish this James from all other Jameses in the world?*

Synopsis (inside book jacket). Comment that to find out in more detail what the book is about, you'd probably turn to the inside of the book jacket. You might be asking yourself such questions as, *Who was this James writing to? What circumstances precipitated the writing of the letter? Do the issues involved bear any significance for me today?* Ask the group to answer these questions one at a time. Encourage them to respond in detail to the questions, but only write a summarizing phrase on the chalkboard for each point made (see chalkboard 1).

Table of Contents. You may incorporate this topic with the previous one when the discussion moves to the subject matter of James' letter. Show MTM-1 at that time, explaining that this will be the outline for our study of the Book of James.

Biographical Notes. Comment that once you have a pretty good idea of what topics James covered in his letter, you may wonder what made this man qualified to speak authoritatively on such weighty matters. Ask the group, *If you turned to the back of the book jacket to read the biographical notes on James, the author, what information would you expect to find?*

Publisher/Editor. Comment as follows: "There is one aspect about the Book of James that makes it unique among most books: the One responsible for editing and publishing the first printing was God. It is for this reason we are going to spend several weeks studying this short book, expecting that

Chalkboard 1
Use for discussion of background to Book of James.

TITLE: <u>Epistle of James</u>: a Handbook on Mature Christian Living
AUTHOR: James, the brother of the Lord
BOOK JACKET SYNOPSIS:
    Letter written to Christian Jews
    Jews scattered by persecution
    Problems in personal lives (name some)
    Problems in church fellowship (name some)
    Same problems today: immaturity
TABLE OF CONTENTS: (Show MTM-1)
BIOGRAPHICAL NOTES:
    Brother of the Lord
    Converted after Jesus' resurrection
    Leader of Jerusalem church
    Spiritual qualities (name some)
    Jewish
    Married
    Martyred
PUBLISHER/EDITOR: God

when we have finished, our lives will be different in some way. For we know that 'the Word of God is living and active . . . and able to judge the thoughts and intentions of the heart' (Heb. 4:12, NASB).

2. "For those of us who like 'How to' books and articles, the author suggests five 'How to's' for getting the most out of this study" (display MTM-2, revealing only one point and accompanying illustration at a time).

"Be born again." Take this time to explain the plan of salvation. Stress that it is impossible to grow to maturity before one is born, both in the physical and spiritual realms. Ask anyone who has any questions about this or who is not sure of his salvation to see you after the session.

"Honestly examine your life in the mirror of God's Word." Ask, *How is God's Word like a mirror to us? What part does honesty play in our self-examination?*

"Obey what God teaches." Ask, *Why is it important to make the decision to obey God even before we know what He wants us to do?*

"Be prepared for extra trials and testings." Have someone recount the incident from the text which is illustrated on the MTM. Stress the author's point that "whenever we are serious about spiritual growth, the Enemy gets serious about opposing us." No one likes the idea of having *extra* trials and temptations; most of us probably feel we have enough as it is. Ask, *What compensations do we have for coping with the extra trials when they come? Why is it important not to "retreat" in the midst of the conflict? How can we prepare ourselves before the trials come?* One way to prepare ourselves is to get extra prayer support. Take a few minutes at this time to have everyone find another person from the group to be his prayer partner for the remaining weeks in the study.

"Measure growth by the Word of God." Have the group turn to the back of their texts where the author listed 12 questions to help us evaluate where we are in our spiritual lives, based on the Book of James. Ask each one to mark with pen or pencil one or two questions which represent areas of his life where growth is needed. Explain that no one has reached ultimate perfection in any area, but if we are honest with ourselves, we can probably see that our need to grow is greater in certain areas than others.

Anticipation

For the next session, ask the group to read James 1:2-12 each day, and to read chapter 2 of the text. Have them jot down on paper instances of trying situations they encounter each day.

Turning Trials into Triumphs | *Text, Chapter 2*

Session Goals
1. To learn the four imperatives for gaining victory in trial situations.
2. To consider the motivation necessary to put them into practice.

Preparation
Throughout the remainder of the study, keep a record of the testings you are confronted with and how you react to each one. This record may be an aid in your own spiritual growth, and perhaps a source for personal illustrations, when appropriate, during the study sessions.

Read James 1:2-12 each day and study chapter 2 of the text, outlining or underlining key ideas. Obtain a woven rug (or a crewel work picture), and prepare chalkboard 2. To make a reminder card for each group member, write or type the lesson's four key words—Count, Know, Let, and Ask—on a heartshape cut from red construction paper.

Presentation
Begin the session by informally asking the group how long their "trial list" (assigned from Session 1) is. Ask if the list is longer or shorter than they expected it to be. Divide class members into buzz groups, having each group compile two lists of trials that a Christian might expect to encounter. Ask a reporter from each group to head one list "Large Trials" and the other list "Small Trials." Explain that while it is difficult to overlook a large trial in our lives, it is sometimes easy to let the small trials come and go without ever recognizing them as trials and consequently, opportunities to grow. Encourage each person to share with his group some of the trying situations he encountered during that week.

After 5 or 10 minutes, ask the group to reassemble. Display the front and back of a woven rug and ask, *What comparison can be made between the trials you just listed and this woven rug?* Comment that because God can weave these "varicolored trials" into something of beauty in our lives, we need to learn how to make them work for us—to "turn trials into triumphs."

Show MTM-3 and discuss each point as follows:

1. *"Count"—A Joyful Attitude.* Ask, *What relationship exists between a person's values and his attitude toward trials?* Write on the chalkboard in one column: comfort, material/physical, present. In another column write: character, spiritual, future. Ask those group members who are parents, which column they think best represents the values their children would hold most important. Ask for one or two examples to substantiate their replies. Summarize this point by explaining that in order to have a

joyful attitude during trials, we may need to examine and rethink some of our values in view of God's desire that we be *mature* Christians.

2. *"Know"—An Understanding Mind.* Ask, *When Satan attempts to bring out the worst in us through trials, with what facts can we guard our minds from defeat?* Write their responses on the board. Incorporate the following questions in the discussion of those facts. *How does testing work for us? How would you define patience? Why do you think the author states that patience is the key to every other blessing? What part does Bible study play in growing in patience?*

3. *"Let"—A Surrendered Will.* Use chalkboard 2 for Neighbor Nudging. Assign a question to every two or three persons just as they are seated so that moving around will not be necessary. Ask each small group to find the answer to their question from the text and in several minutes present both the question and answer to the rest of the class.

4. *"Ask"—A Believing Heart.* Have everyone read James 1:5-8, considering the following questions: *When faced with a trial, what should I pray for and how should I pray?* Discuss these questions, adding that we can use these same guidelines as we pray for others, particularly our prayer partners within the study group.

Draw attention to the heading "For Love's Sake" on MTM-3 and ask, *In James 1:12, what relationship do you see between enduring temptation and loving the Lord? What do you do everyday that is motivated by love for someone? Do the difficult tasks seem easier because love is involved?*

Summarize by saying that we can view testing situations as opportunities

Chalkboard 2
Use for Neighbor Nudging activity.

A SURRENDERED WILL

1. How would you define the word "perfect" as it is used in James 1:4?

2. What is God's goal for us as Christians?

3. What are the three "works" involved in the maturing process?

4. How do Abraham, Joseph, Moses, and the disciples illustrate the "sanctification before service" principle?

5. What is God's spiritual weaning process?

6. How do verses 9-11 of James 1 illustrate the process of spiritual weaning?

to return our love in a very tangible way to the One who loves us more than anyone else ever could. Close by having prayer partners share requests and pray with each other.

Anticipation

Hand out reminder cards (see *Presentation*), asking the group to put them someplace where they will be noticed at least once a day. Assign the reading of James 1:13-18 and chapter 3 of the text. Assign book report (see Session 3).

How to Handle Temptation / *Text, Chapter 3*

Session Goals

1. To understand how testing can lead to temptation.
2. To learn what three barriers deter us from sin.
3. To recognize that no Christian has to yield to temptation.

Preparation

Read James 1:13-18 each day. Read chapter 3 of the text, carefully outlining on note cards the key points supporting each of the three main considerations: God's judgment, God's goodness, and God's presence within. Gather paper, pencils, and colored pens for the first activity. Prepare chalkboard 3 and a poster of the excuse phrases list (see *Presentation, #3*). Obtain the book *In Two Minds* by Os Guinness (Downers Grove: InterVarsity Press, 1976) and give the topic assignment (based on chapter 16) to a volunteer: "What to Do When God Does Not Seem Good."

Presentation

1. Begin the session by asking if the heart reminder cards were helpful during the week. Allow time for informal sharing.

Display MTM-1 to review briefly what has already been discussed in the study and how it relates to the whole theme and outline. Ask, *What is the distinction between testing on the outside and temptation on the inside?* Display and explain MTM-4 to supplement group response. Introduce the three barriers that deter us from sin.

2. Continue as follows: "You probably noticed in your reading for this session that both James and Dr. Wiersbe made frequent use of word pictures to help us better understand and apply various truths and principles." Refer to chalkboard 3.

"Take a few minutes right now to graphically illustrate (sketch, cartoon, diagram) some truth which impressed you as you read your assignment. (Hand out paper and pencils as you explain.) You don't need to worry about the artistic quality of your work. You may use any of the ideas listed on the chalkboard or you may use an original idea. Be prepared to relate the truth illustrated in your drawing to one of the three sin barriers."

Write the three barriers on the chalkboard (God's judgment, goodness, and Presence within) for the group's easy reference. You may also want to prepare a drawing of your own to show group members what they are to do, or you may use MTM-4 for the same purpose. Allow 5 to 10 minutes for this activity. Begin discussion by asking those people whose drawings relate to the first sin barrier to show and explain their illustrations. If your group will be so large that illustrations will be difficult to see for many people, subdivide the group and appoint another discussion leader for each group prior to this session. Be prepared to briefly summarize all the key points presented in this section (refer to your outline), whether or not the point has been illustrated with a drawing. Proceed in the same manner for discussion of the last two sin barriers.

3. As the author considers the second barrier to sin, he states, "Once we start to doubt God's goodness, we will be attracted to Satan's offers; and the natural desires within will reach out for his bait." Incorporate into the discussion of the second barrier a report on the topic, *What to Do When God Does Not Seem Good,* based on the book *In Two Minds,* chapter 16. In summary of the second barrier, ask everyone to think of two or three gifts from the Lord for which they are most thankful and which could serve as symbols of God's great goodness to them.

Following discussion of the third barrier, show the group a poster or transparency with the following phrases written on it:

"I couldn't help myself. The devil made me do it."

"I'm not perfect, and I won't be until I get to heaven."

"I just couldn't stand it (a trying circumstance) any longer."

"The guy (the target of a sinful act) deserved it anyway."

"I was in a bad mood."

Ask, *How would you title this group of phrases?* (For instance, Excuses for Yielding to Sin). *Can you think of any other excuses Christians sometimes make for yielding to sin?* Add responses to the list. *Why is each one invalid?* Read 1 Corinthians 10:13. Stress in summary that because of God's presence within us we *always* have the power to win the victory over temptation and sin. When we don't win, the problem is one of will rather than ability.

Anticipation

Read James 1:19-27 in several translations and chapter 4 of the text.

WORD PICTURES

Steam boiler	Lights/Shadows
Master/Servant	Satan's "bargains"
Baiting a trap	1st birth/2nd birth
Baiting a hook	Firstfruits
Birth of a Baby	Crown/Coffin
Child/Adult	
Gift/Giving	

Chalkboard 3
Use as a reference to the word pictures employed by James and the author of the text.

Quit Kidding Yourself | *Text, Chapter 4*

Session Goals
1. To learn how to identify spiritual self-deception in our own lives.
2. To understand the important role the Word of God plays in the process of our spiritual maturity.

Preparation

Read James 1:19-27 each day and study chapter 4 of the text, outlining or underlining important ideas as you read. Be sure to answer all the discussion questions in the *Leader's Guide* yourself so that you can anticipate where discussions are or should be heading during the class session. Prepare or gather teaching aids: a packet of seeds, discussion question cards, chalkboard 4, and literature on personal Bible study.

Presentation

Review the previous session by displaying MTM-4. To introduce this session's topic, comment that many times we sin, not because Satan deceives us but because we deceive ourselves. Ask, *From James 1:19-27, how were some of the early Christians deceiving themselves? Do we see this same type of problem in the Christian church today? In what ways?*

Ask, *If one is self-deceived, how can he, being both the deceiver and the deceived, become aware of the problem?* To illustrate and perhaps clarify the question, ask, *Have you ever left the house in the morning in such a rush that you forgot to check the mirror before leaving—only to find later that your socks didn't match?* State: "You probably didn't realize the problem until someone else pointed it out or until you saw yourself in a mirror." Make a comparison between this situation and how the Bible acts as a mirror to reveal sin involving self-deception. Have someone read aloud the paragraph discussing this, on page 55 of the text.

Discuss the three responsibilities we have toward God's Word as follows. Use chalkboard 4 to introduce each responsibility.

Receive the Word. Hold up a seed and ask, *If this seed is to germinate, mature, and produce this delicious food* (or these beautiful flowers)—hold up seed packet with picture of mature plant—*what has to be done with the soil before and after planting? If the Word of God is going to take root in our lives and produce the good fruit of maturity, what kind of heart preparation needs to be done?* Write responses on the chalkboard.

Comment that we usually hear James 1:19 applied to our relationships with people. Ask, *How does it also apply to our relationship with the Bible, God's Word?*

Practice the Word. Divide the class into four discussion groups. Write the four discussion questions below on separate cards, giving one of these questions to each group:

1. How is God's Word like a mirror for examination?
2. What are some mistakes people make as they look into God's Word?
3. How is God's Word like a mirror for restoration?
4. How is God's Word like a mirror for transformation?

The second and third discussion questions for all four of the groups will be the same: *What are some problems you encounter when trying to establish and maintain a daily Bible study time? What practical solutions can we find for these problems?* After 5 to 10 minutes, ask each group to share its findings. Complete discussion on questions 1-4 above before proceeding to the group discussion on the last two questions.

Share the Word. Use the brainstorming method of discussion to answer this question: *Name some specific, practical ways that Christians can "share the Word" in speech, service, and separation.* Write "Speech," "Service," and "Separation" on chalkboard 4 as column headings and record responses as they are given. Encourage the group to be creative and specific. Challenge each person to pick at least one of the suggestions given and practice it in the coming week to "share the Word."

Summarize by noting that one cannot receive, practice, and share the Word without reading and studying it first. Try to obtain some good books, booklets, or magazine articles on how to start a personal Bible study time, and make these available on loan to group members. For assistance, check with your church librarian or local Christian bookstore. To close, allow time for prayer partners to pray with each other.

Anticipation

Announce that the next session will deal with Christian maturity and personal relationships. Assign James 2:1-13 and chapter 5 of the text.

<table>
<tr><td colspan="3">Three Responsibilities Toward the Word
1. Receive the Word
2. Practice the Word
3. Share the Word by means of:</td></tr>
<tr><td>Speech</td><td>Service</td><td>Separation</td></tr>
<tr><td></td><td></td><td></td></tr>
</table>

Chalkboard 4
Use to introduce three responsibilities we have toward God's Word.

Rich Man, Poor Man / *Text, Chapter 5*

Session Goal

To show how our beliefs about God and His Word should control our attitudes and behavior toward other people.

Preparation

Read James 2:1-13 each day and study chapter 5 of the text. Carefully outline the important ideas under each doctrine presented and write this outline on note cards for your use during group discussion. Be sure you can explain how each doctrine relates to interpersonal relationships, and how the session goal above relates to the author's outline subheading for this section, "Faith and Love." Prepare chalkboard 5 and gather materials needed.

Presentation

1. Ask the group members if they were able to "share the Word" in some way during the past week. Allow time for informal sharing.

2. Display MTM-1 and ask, *As you face the small or large trials you encounter each day, are you finding it easier to be patient—to count, know, let, and ask? In your Bible study times this week, has God's Word been like a mirror to you?* Give a brief overview of the second characteristic of the mature Christian and explain how this session's subject, "Relationships with People," relates to it.

To introduce the topic, comment as follows: "Isn't it interesting that *other* people are never as easy to get along with as *we* are? Wherever we go, we find people that irritate us for one reason or another. Sometimes we can avoid these people completely, but more often than not, such a person is your boss or co-worker, your next-door neighbor, an in-law, or one who works on the same church committee as you do."

Display MTM-5 and ask, *What characteristics about certain people make it difficult for you to associate with them?* Write responses in the bricks of the wall. Ask, *What are some other walls built up between people that may not necessarily be a problem for you (for instance, the issues James was addressing in chapter 2)?* Write these responses on the bricks as well. Some possible responses are: coarse language, rude, smokes, demanding, pushy, superior attitude, talks too much, nosey, different political or theological opinions, not educated, personality conflicts, dresses shabbily, offensive odors, different race, not in same social circle.

3. Comment that in James 2, four doctrines are cited to show us a different perspective of interpersonal relationships and their inherent problems. Divide the class into four discussion groups and ask them to consider the questions on chalkboard 5.

Call time and be prepared to summarize or add important ideas after each group has contributed.

Display MTM-5 again, calling attention to the caption. Write on the chalkboard or on a poster: "Our beliefs (faith) should control our behavior (love)." Explain that we would all readily affirm our faith in the doctrines we have just discussed (point to four questions on the chalkboard). Yet our attitudes and behavior do not always reflect this faith. The author of the text made a startling statement about this apparent inconsistency: "We only believe as much of the Bible as we practice." Ask, *What is your reaction to this statement? Can you explain further what he meant by it?*

4. For personal application, ask the group members to think of one person they come in contact with often, but have a difficult time getting along with. Hand out paper to each person as you give instructions: "Write that person's name or initials at the top of the page. Papers will not be turned in. Divide the paper into two columns. Head one column: Even though you ________________. Head the other column: I can love you because ________________."

Allow several minutes for everyone to fill in the columns. Close in prayer, asking God to give us the will and power to act in love to the person named on each paper, just as God loved us when we were and are unlovely.

Anticipation

Comment that James' statement, "Faith without works is dead," (2:17,

Chalkboard 5
Use for discussion of four doctrines.

Which Four Doctrines Do These Questions Explore?

1. How should the doctrine of the deity of Christ affect our relationships with people? What does it mean to look at people through the eyes of Christ?

2. How should the doctrine of the grace of God affect our relationships with people?

3. The "Royal Law" in the Word of God _commands_ us to love our neighbor. Why can love be commanded of us? Define Christian love.

4. What aspects of our behavior toward other people will God judge? By what criteria will God judge?

     Lesson material continued after MTM inserts

Instructions for Victor Multi-use
Transparency Masters

As mentioned in the *Introduction to This Study* (*Guide,* p. 6), this removable center section provides 14 Victor Multi-use Transparency Masters as important helps to your teaching this course. How transparencies can be made from them will be explained and instructions will be given for the specific use of each chalkboard or visual aid.

With educators' recognition of the teaching value of visual aids—even for adults—the Victor Multi-use Transparency Masters in this guide have been designed to give you maximum teaching help. They are numbered consecutively (MTM-1—MTM-14) and are coded to refer to both the guide and the text page numbers to which the illustrations relate. (The abbreviation **G**, followed by a number or numbers, refers to the page numbers in the leader's guide; the abbreviation **T**, followed by a number or numbers, refers to the page numbers in the textbook being studied.)

Some of the best visual aids available today are transparencies for overhead projection. Effective, creative teachers increasingly use transparencies to enliven class sessions and to transmit vital information to the mind through the eye-gate. Many churches already have overhead projectors, and each church should consider purchasing at least one, or one for each department. Ready-to-use transparencies are available and are becoming more so in the Christian education market, but they are expensive. However, you can make your own transparencies inexpensively through the use of transparency masters such as the ones in this guide.

Mechanics

Open up each of the staples carefully and pull out the seven sheets of illustrations and the one sheet of instructions. Close the staples again to keep your leader's guide together. Straighten out the seven illustration sheets by running a finger along the crease and file flat in a regular file folder (usually 9″ x 11¾″). Leave the instructions folded for easier reference (they are labeled as pages a, b, c, and d) and file with the transparency masters.

Making Transparencies from Masters

You can make transparencies in at least four ways:

1. *Thermal copier* (an infrared heat transfer process such as 3M's Thermofax). It is probably the fastest, most convenient, and best-known method. Simply pass the master with the appropriate film on top of the master through the copying machine (at the correct setting).

2. *Electrostatic process* (such as Xerox). Because of paper feeding requirements in these machines, care must be taken to have the correct film for the proper machine. Check before using. Also, the glass must be absolutely clean or all the dirt and dust particles will be picked up. The color on the MTM will come out gray.

3. *Photo-reflex process* (sometimes called the diffusion-transfer process). A wet process involving the exposure of a sheet of negative paper, placing it in contact with a sheet of positive paper or transparency film, and sending it through a processing machine (such as produced by Kodak, Agfa-Gevaert, and GAF Corporation).

4. *Trace your own on a transparency film.* (See below.)

Don't give up if your church does not have a copying machine. You likely live within a short distance of a machine. Try your public library, a school, or a secretarial service office (Copying or Duplicating Service in your Yellow Pages). Or maybe there's a machine at your office, or at a friend's. Usually arrangements can be made, either paying for the film or bringing your own.

You must be careful to have the right film for the right machine. To do so, first determine the type of copier that is available to you or to your friends. Then purchase the correct film from a local supplier (if not available with the machine), either an office supply house or a school supply company. If neither of these is available to you, order *A Teacher's Guide to Overhead Projection* (1969, Technifax Education Division, Holyoke, Mass. 01040), which is an excellent manual describing the production and operation of transparencies and includes the company's descriptions and prices, or *The Overhead System: Production, Implementation, and Utilization* (1972, University of Texas Visual Instruction Bureau, Drawer W, University Station, Austin, Texas 78712), which includes a valuable appendix of addresses for sources of equipment and materials.

An alternate use for the transparency masters in this guide is for you to trace your own transparencies from the masters. With minimum artistic ability required, you can place a sheet of film over the master (the sheet should be at least 10″ x 7″) and trace the major part of the illlustration. Exactness is not necessary and stick figures (as in the chalkboards) can be traced over the printed figures; lettering can be done separately. (For best results use .005 acetate or .003 polyester either in 8½″ x 11″ sheets or in a roll that can be cut to appropriate size.)

To write on the transparencies, use a grease pencil, preferably white, or a felt-tip marking pen. The former is harder to erase and does not look as neat as the latter. Take care, however, in purchasing felt-tip marking pens, for there are a number of different kinds on the market. For transparencies you must have either erasable or nonpermanent if you wish to reuse the film (these wash off with water or a damp cloth quite easily), or permanent if you want to reuse the same visual aid. You may want to make the basic image with the permanent pen and add other material as needed with the washable one.

A further advantage of tracing your own transparencies is that you can make overlays. You expose only one part of the illustration; then, as the discussion progresses you expose the rest of it in parts or sections.

Other Uses of Transparency Masters

1. *Ditto Masters.* Another use to which the transparency masters may be put is making Ditto masters from which you can run off material for

b

b.   Faith and works   14-26

3.   He has power over his tongue   1-18

4.   He is a peacemaker, not a troublemaker   1-17

5.   He is prayerful in troubles

      a.   Economic troubles   1-9

      b.   Physical troubles   10-16

      c.   National troubles   17-18

      d.   Church troubles   19-20

How to get the most out of this study:

1.

Be born again

2.

Honestly examine your
life in the mirror of

COUNT
Have a joyful attitude

KNOW
Have an understanding mind

LET
Have a surrendered will

ASK
Have a believing heart

MTM-4 (G-13,15)

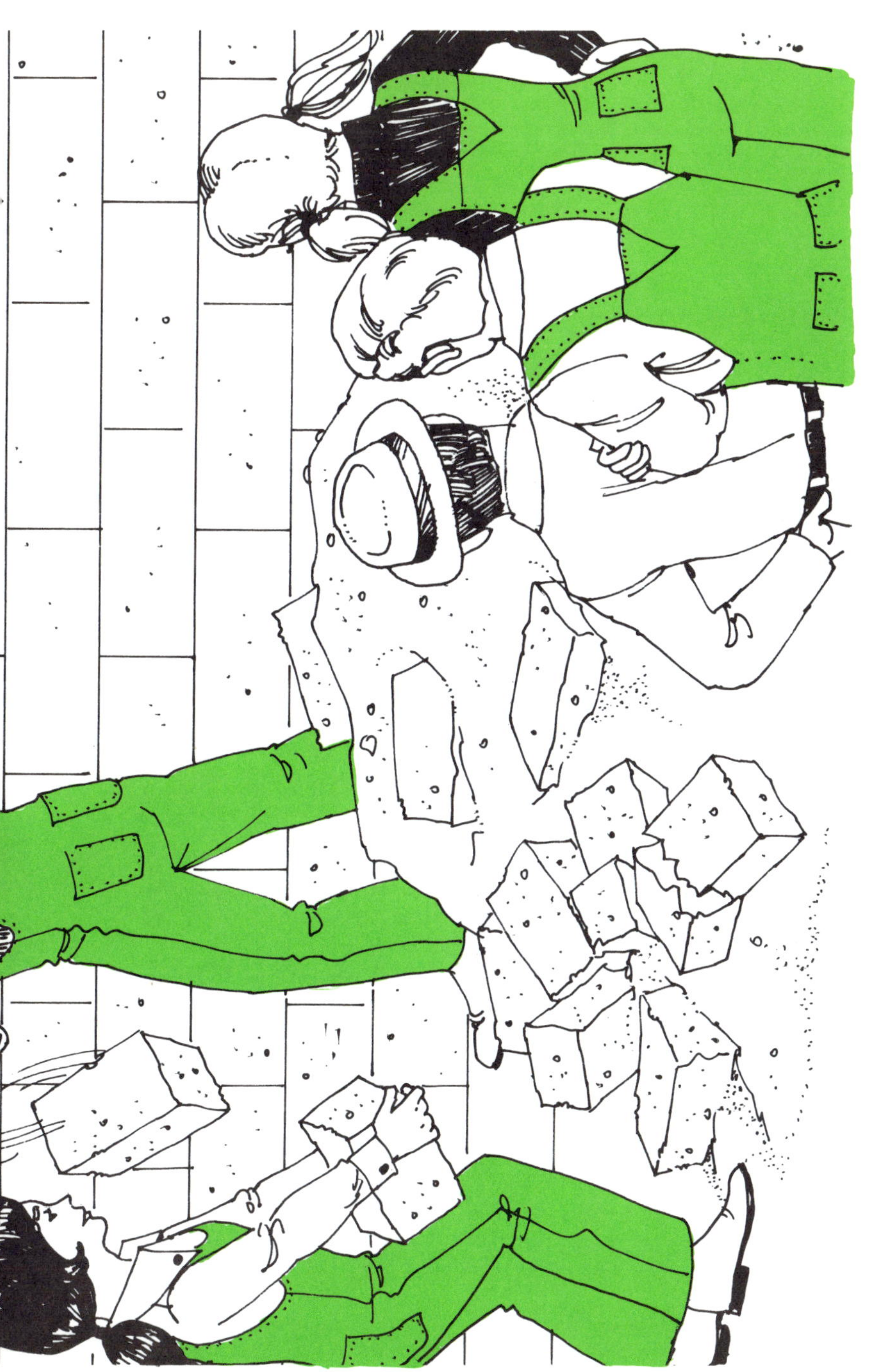

CREEDS OF FAITH

THE CREED OF DEAD FAITH

1. We believe the Christian doctrine intellectually.

2. We believe that our words are sufficient evidence of our faith.

3. We believe our faith insures us of eternal life.

THE CREED OF DEVILS

MTM-6 (G-20, 21)

GOD'S POWER CELL
POWER TO DIRECT POSITIVELY(+)
POWER TO DELIGHT
HELL'S POWER CELL
POWER TO DIRECT NEGATIVELY(−)
POWER TO DESTROY

Who-o-o is wise and understanding among you? Let him show it by his good life, by deeds done in the humility of wisdom.

MTM-8 (G-25)

"Not my will, but Thine be done"

2.   DRAW NEAR TO GOD

Confess sin and ask for cleansing

Resist the devil

"Cleanse your hands and purify your hearts"

3.   HUMBLE YOURSELVES BEFORE GOD

Recognize the seriousness of sin

Deal with disobedience

"A broken and a contrite heart, O God, Thou wilt not despise"

MTM-10 (G-29)

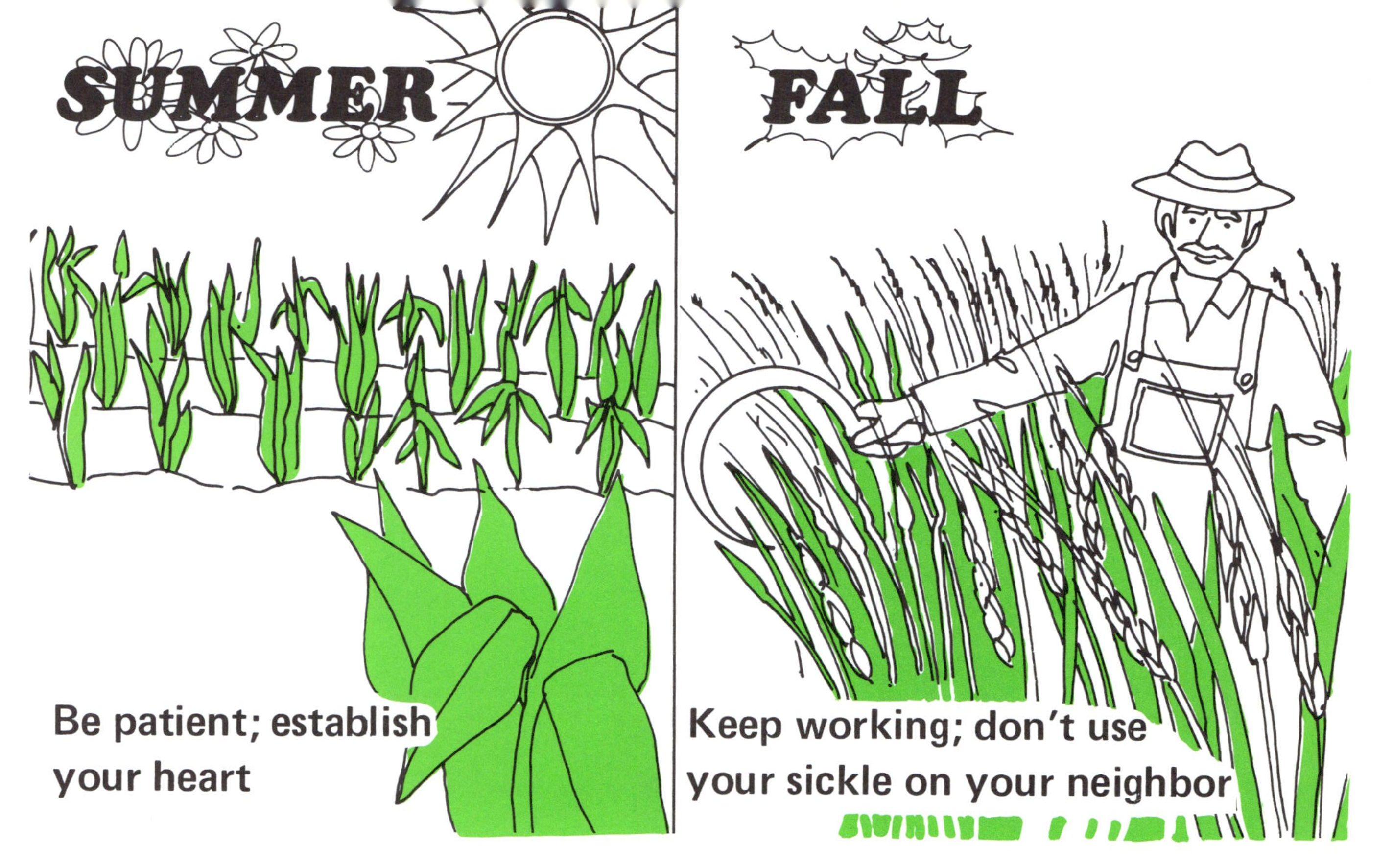

SUMMER
FALL
Be patient; establish your heart
Keep working; don't use your sickle on your neighbor

For the effectual fervent prayer of a righteous man availeth much . . .
sick
nation
church

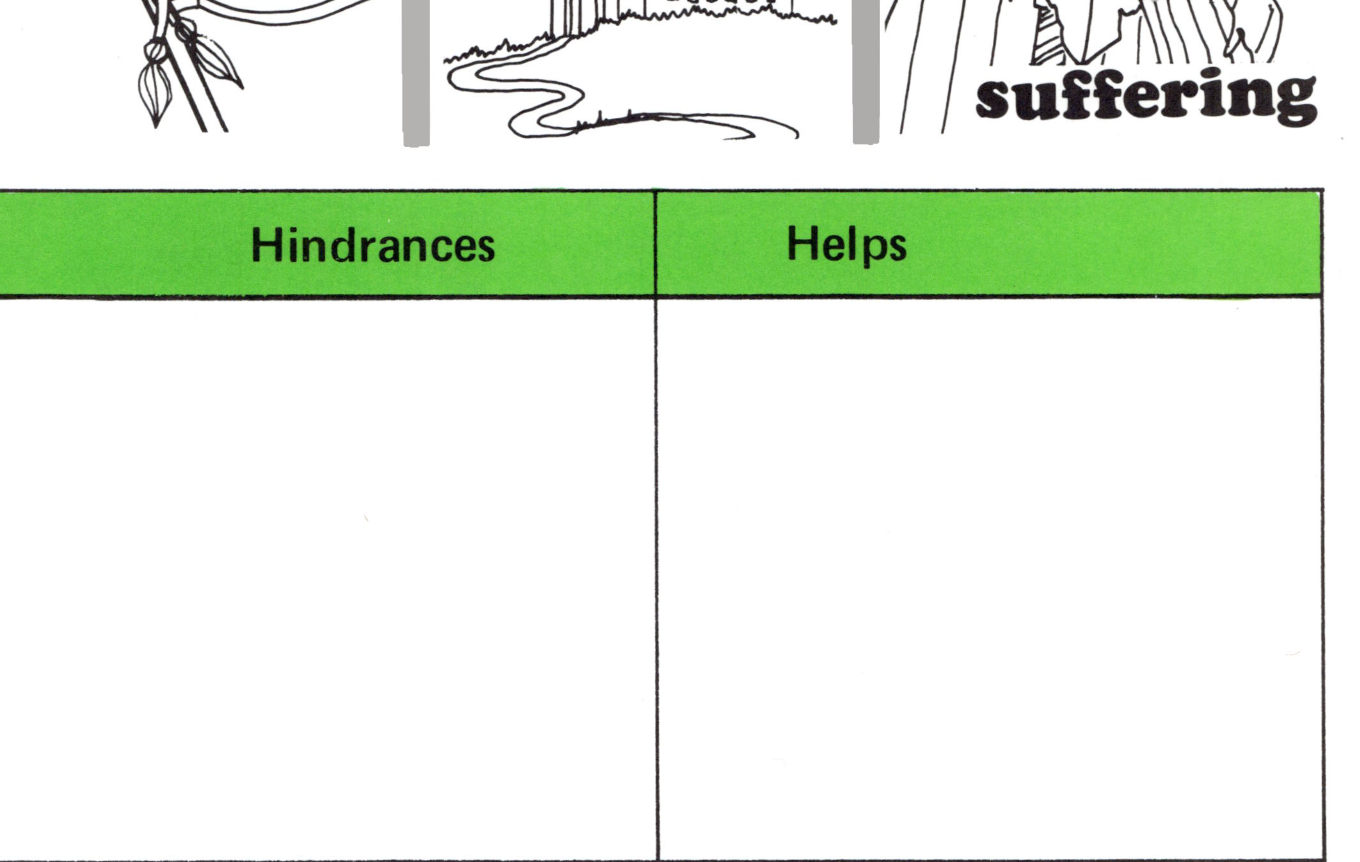

Hindrances	Helps

God is producing a harvest in our lives

MTM-11   (G-33)

like a living body

DO FROM
THE HEART

PROVE

UNDERSTAND

KNOW

a growing experience

PEACE TREATY
TERMS OF SETTLEMENT:
1.   SUBMIT TO GOD
Unconditional surrender is the only way to complete

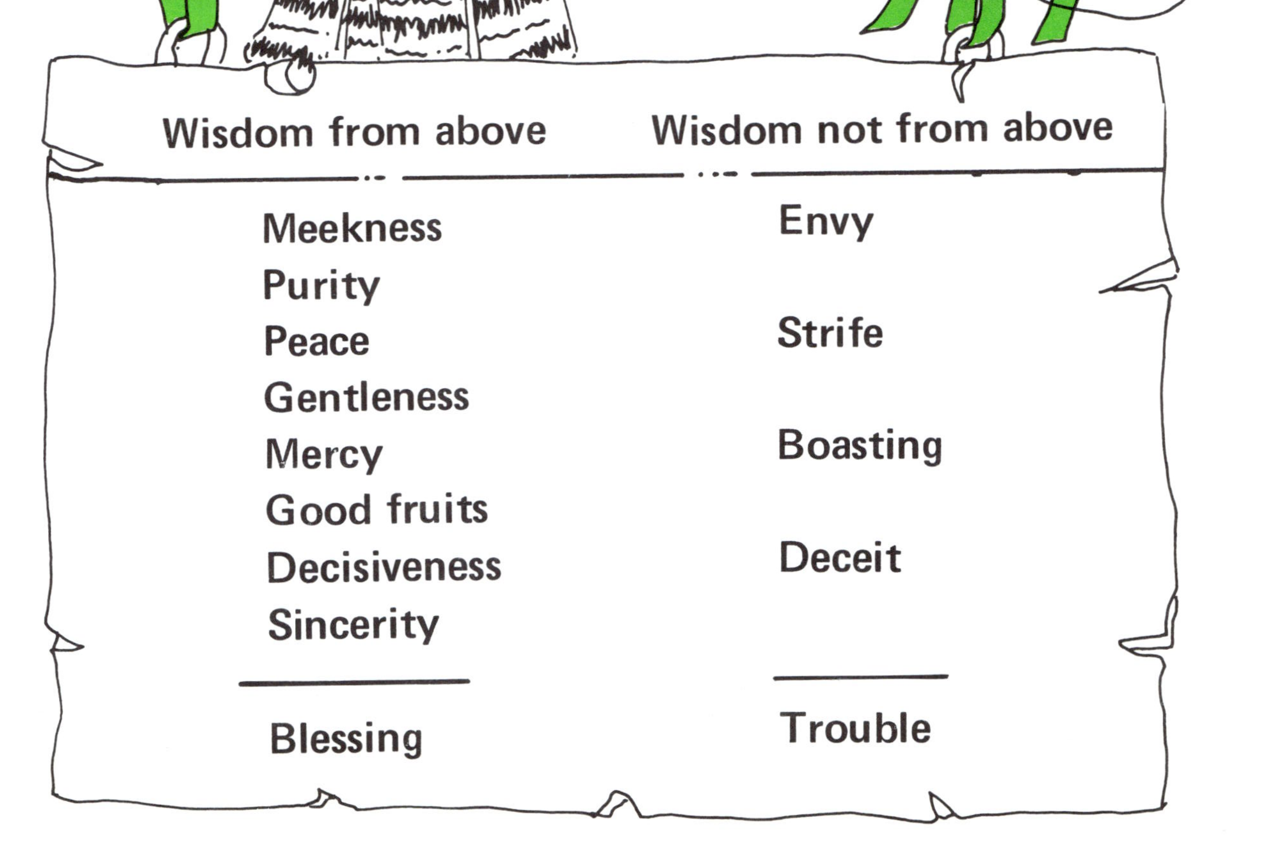

Wisdom from above
Wisdom not from above
Meekness
Purity
Peace
Gentleness
Mercy
Good fruits
Decisiveness
Sincerity
Blessing
Envy
Strife
Boasting
Deceit
Trouble

"Set a watch O Lord, before my mouth, keep the door of my lips. Incline not my heart to any evil thing" (Ps. 141:3-4).

We believe in the existence of God and the deity of His Son, Jesus Christ.

2. We believe in the judgment of God and shudder as we think about it.

THE CREED OF DYNAMIC FAITH

1. We believe in the Word of God as the basis of our faith.

2. We believe with our intellect, emotions. and will.

3. We believe that our faith results in changed lives, and that the changes will be evident by our actions (works).

FAITH AND LOVE
BREAK DOWN
THE WALLS
BETWEEN PEOPLE

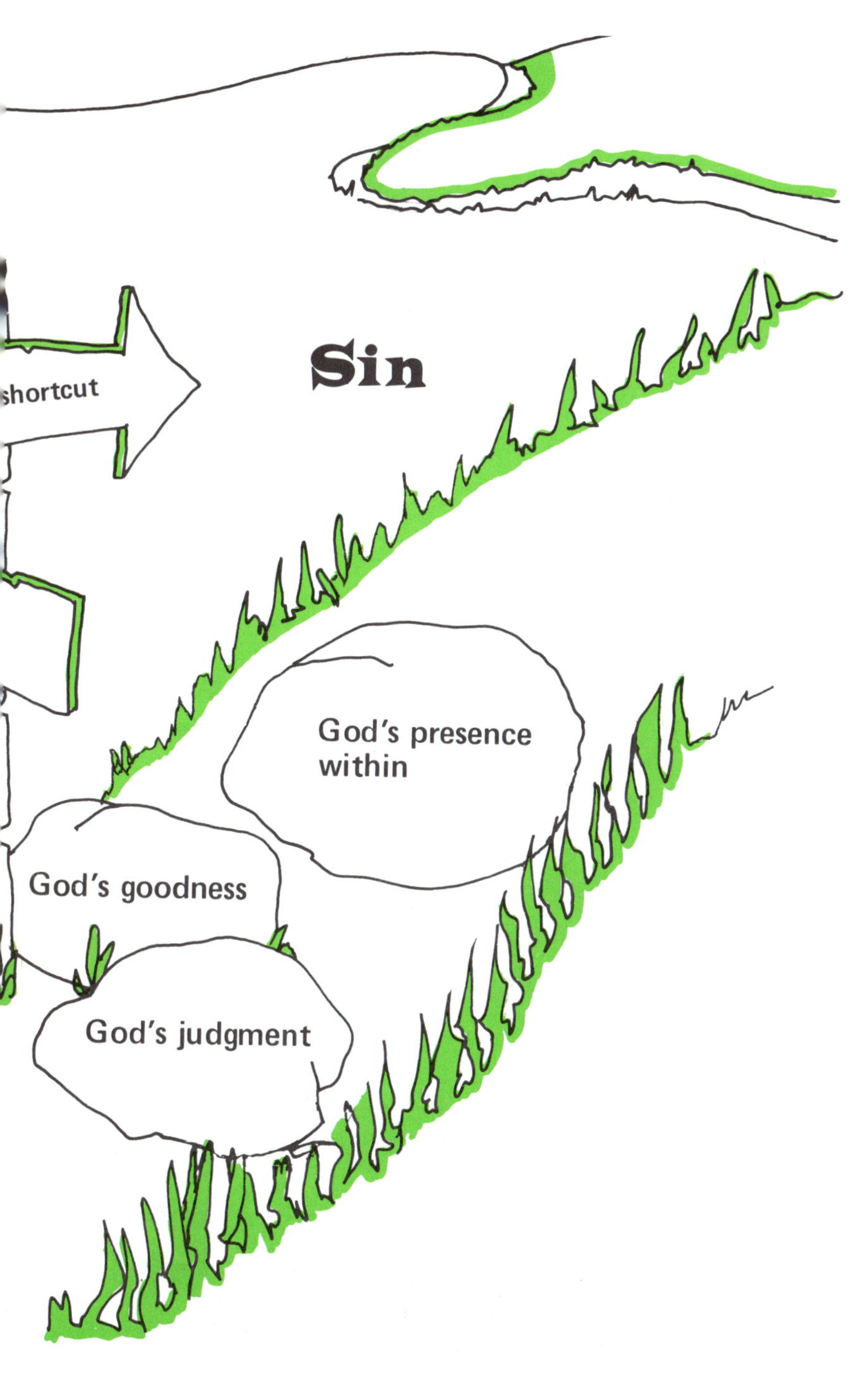

shortcut
Sin
God's presence within
God's goodness
God's judgment

FOR LOVE'S SAKE
TURN TRIALS
INTO TRIUMPHS

3.

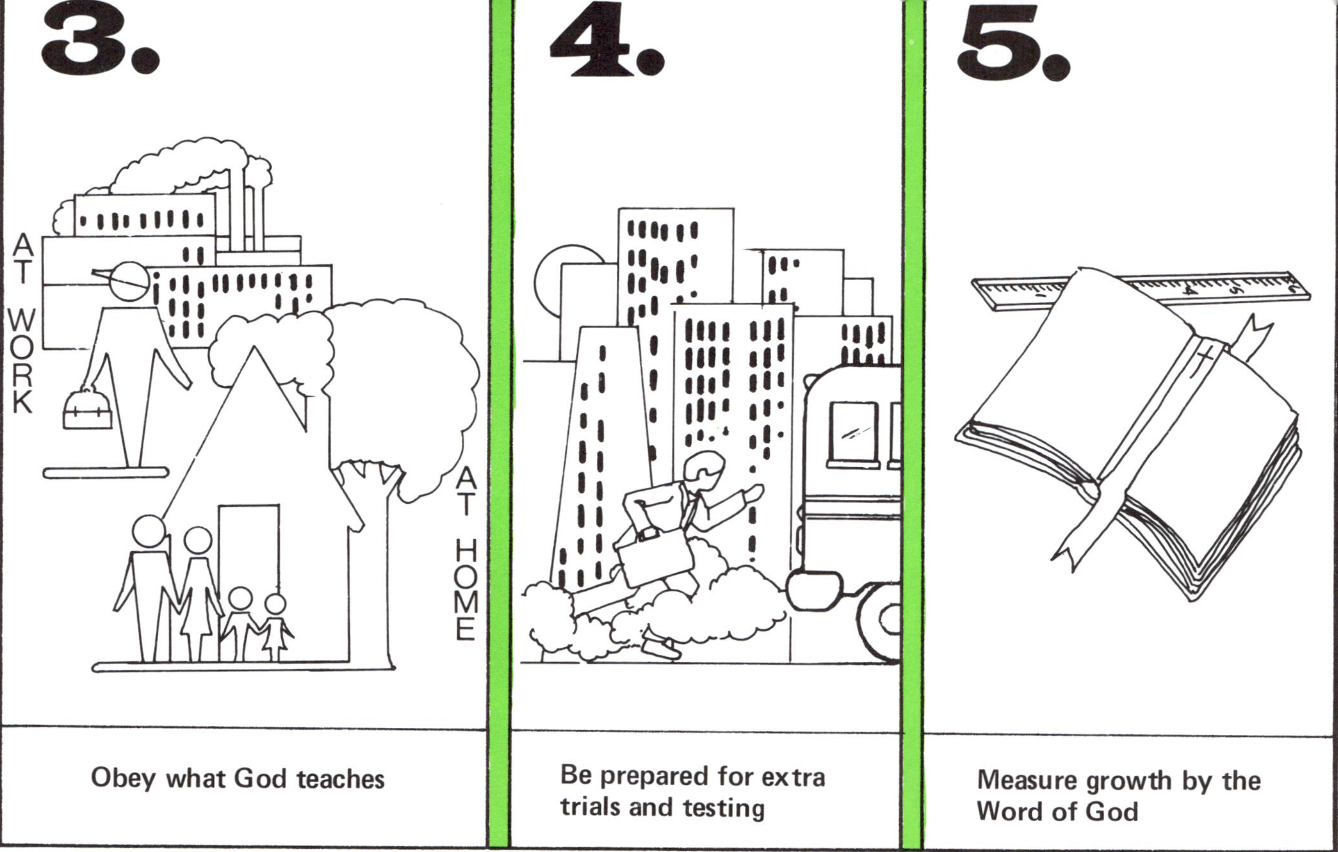

Obey what God teaches

4.

Be prepared for extra
trials and testing

5.

Measure growth by the
Word of God

Marks of a Mature Christian

(from the Book of James)

Chapter		Verses
1.	He is patient in testing	
	a. Trials on the outside	1-12
	b. Temptations on the inside	13-27
2.	He practices the truth	
	a. Faith and love	1-13

each member of your class. The basic process is the same as that used for overhead transparencies. The transparency master has a thermal spirit master placed over it and is then run through a thermal copier (such as a Thermofax machine). From the master as many copies as needed are then made on any Ditto or spirit machine. If a Thermofax machine is not available, then the transparency master may be traced or copied onto a Ditto master or mimeograph, run off on the respective machines, and copies distributed to the class.

2. *Visuals.* For small classes or home Bible classes, the transparency masters may be used just as they are as visual aids to the lesson. It would be helpful to tape them or glue them to a piece of cardboard (making copies of the illustration on the back) and then prop up the visual against some books or with a homemade prop behind it. You are then free to refer to it during the lecture or discussion as it stands on the table near you.

3. *Chalkboards.* You may also use the transparency masters just as you do the other chalkboards in the guide. Simply copy the illustration onto a chalkboard or flip chart and use it as needed in your presentation (see *General Preparation,* third and fourth paragraphs, *Guide,* p. 4).

The Use of Color

In all of the methods discussed above (except that of Visuals) the colors on the transparency masters are to serve as guides to the teacher in coloring his transparencies, dittoes, or chalkboards. The colors will not reproduce in the various processes (except in the Xerox, where the color turns out to be a gray shading), but will serve as guides for emphasis and distinction as the teacher colors in his transparencies.

Materials

The following is a partial list of materials necessary for the maximum use of transparencies, either through a mechanical copying process or homemade.

1. *Transparency Film.* 3M Corporation makes clear transparency film for the infrared process, 100 sheets to a box. LABELON Projection Transparencies—Infrared, 100 sheets to a box (TR-85). Also available in kits, which include clear and colored acetates, pens, frames, grease pencils, and instructions.

2. *Ditto Masters.* 3M Corporation; Klean Write KEM-FAX Spirit Masters (No. 321-D); and Heyer's Thermal Spirit Masters (No. 450 Purple).

3. *Pens.* These are available in many colors, both permanent and washable (but make sure that the kind you get will write on acetate).

Permanent—Sanford's (Bellwood, Ill. 60104) Vis-à-Vis Sharpie Pens; Eberhard Faber's Projectachrome Overhead Projector Markers (permanent); and 3M Visual Products Transparency Marking Pens (permanent).

Washable—Sanford's Vis-à-Vis Visual Aid Pens; Eberhard Faber and 3M clearly marked "non-permanent."

4. *Grease Pencils.* Widely available in any office supply store.

Victor Multiuse Transparency Masters for This Guide

The following are some suggestions for using the transparency masters in this *Leader's Guide* ("G" stands for this guide).

MTM-1 (G-8, 13, 17, 27, 31, 36)—Display as indicated in various sessions to focus on the marks of a mature Christian.

MTM-2 (G-9)—Display, revealing only one point and illustration at a time.

MTM-3 (G-10, 11)—Display and discuss each principle.

MTM-4 (G-13, 15)—Display and explain to supplement group response and as a review.

MTM-5 (G-17, 18)—Display to aid discussion of interpersonal relationships.

MTM-6 (G-20, 21)—Display and present the main ideas under the three kinds of faith.

MTM-7 (G-23, 25)—Display during discussion of the power of the tongue.

MTM-8 (G-25)—Display to summarize main ideas of the discussion on wisdom.

MTM-9 (G-27)—Display to present the "terms of settlement."

MTM-10 (G-29, 30)—Display to aid discussion of the will of God for every Christian.

MTM-11 (G-33)—Display to illustrate how a Christian is like a farmer.

MTM-12 (G-35, 36)—Display to illustrate the value of prayer in a Christian's life.

d.

20 and 26) has been the topic of much theological discussion and contro-
versy for many centuries. We will be taking a closer look at this statement
during the next session.

Ask the group to read James 2:14-26 several times. Try to identify the
three kinds of faith mentioned there before reading the text. Then read
chapter 5 of the text and check your answers.

Instruct group members to conduct a short survey, asking two or three
people, "How would you define religious faith?"

Make the three special assignments as explained in Session 6 (*Prep-
aration*).

False Faith | *Text, Chapter 6*

Session Goals
1. To understand the meaning of true faith and its relationship to works.
2. To determine what kind of faith we possess.

Preparation
Find volunteers for three special presentations. Ask one man to prepare a five-minute narration in the first person on Abraham's life, allowing the greatest amount of time for recounting the incidents of Genesis 15 and 22. Ask one woman to prepare a narration in the first person on Rahab's life from Joshua 2 and 6. Encourage them not only to state facts but to tell how the biblical characters felt in each situation. When no scriptural clues are given about emotions, ask the narrators to imagine how the characters may have felt. Inform them that a Bible dictionary may aid in their preparation.

Ask the third volunteer to prepare a short presentation on the topic, "Abraham and Justification" based on Romans 4. Suggest some good Bible study aids for his use. Tell each volunteer how his presentation fits into the session's progression of ideas.

Do a study on the word "faith" as it is used in the Bible. Some helpful study aids are: a Bible dictionary, concordance, Scofield notes, and a book of word studies in the New Testament.

Study James 2:14-26 and chapter 6 in the text. As you display MTM-6, be prepared to present the main ideas under the three kinds of faith. Prepare chalkboard 6 and gather needed materials.

Presentation
1. Summarize in a couple of sentences what key ideas have been covered thus far in the study and how they each relate to the theme. Ask the group what kind of responses they received to their short surveys on the definition of religious faith. Compile a list of the definitions obtained from the survey, writing each one on the chalkboard. Ask the group to evaluate each definition according to their own understanding of the term. Ask, *If you were to define genuine saving faith, what elements would you include in the definition?* Write responses on the chalkboard.

Comment that there must have been as much confusion and misunderstanding about what faith meant in James' day as there is today. To make himself clear, James distinguished between three kinds of faith.

2. Display MTM-6 and present the three "Creeds of Faith" point by point. Supplement each main point with supportive details or examples from Scripture, the text, your own experience, or your research on faith.

After presenting the "Creed of Dynamic Faith," compare elements of the group's definition of faith with the Creed. Continue by noting that James gives two examples of people who had such faith and that the group is fortunate to have these two people with them today. Ask "Abraham" to speak to the group.

Then ask, *When James referred to Abraham's great works of faith, was he implying that we can work for salvation?* Quickly sketch chalkboard 6 and comment that many people have this concept of salvation. The Apostle Paul wanted us to know that no one can earn salvation, and he used Abraham for his example in Romans 4. Ask that the special report on "Abraham and Justification" be given at this time. Following that report, ask someone to summarize the relationship between faith and works in Abraham's life.

3. State: "James gives us one other example of genuine faith, someone who contrasts with Abraham in almost every respect but one: her faith led her to action." Introduce "Rahab" and ask her to speak.

4. Display MTM-6 again and ask, *Which kind of faith do you have?* Have everyone turn to the end of chapter 6 in the text, where the author lists 10 questions to help us take inventory on the kind of faith we have. Allow time for everyone to read them. Invite those who would like further information on this matter of faith and salvation to see you after the session.

Close by singing or reading the first and last stanzas of the hymn "Faith of Our Fathers."

Anticipation

Announce that the next session will deal with something that reminds us of nuclear energy in that it has such a great potential for both constructive and destructive enterprises. Our subject will be the tongue. Ask the group to read James 3:1-14 several times in various translations, and chapter 7 of the text.

Chalkboard 6
Use to illustrate that salvation is not a matter of our good works outweighing our bad works.

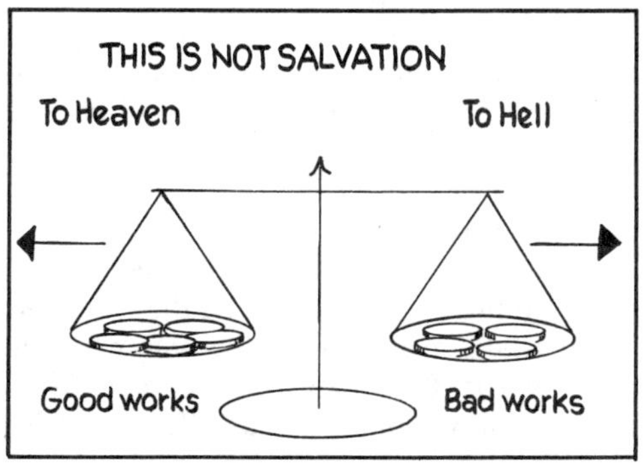

The World's Smallest but Largest Troublemaker

Text, Chapter 7

Session Goals

1. To examine the great potential of the tongue, both for evil and for good.

2. To consider how we may strengthen our own tongue's "power to delight."

Preparation

Ask a Christian counselor, psychiatrist or psychologist in your area to speak at this session on the topic, "How Our Words Affect Others." Express particular interest in his sharing practical suggestions and examples of how to and how not to communicate in interpersonal relationships of various kinds—in the family, at work, in the church, etc. Explain how this topic relates to the session goals and the text material, and inform him that there will be a question-answer period following his presentation. Tell him how long you would like his presentation to be. If the person you contact is unable to come to the session, tape an interview with him asking such questions as: *Based on your experience in dealing with people's problems, how important would you say communication is in establishing good interpersonal relationships? How damaging can our words be to others? What are some reasons people lash out at others with words? Could you suggest some practical ways that we could improve the quality of our communication with others?*

If you are unable to obtain a speaker or interview for the session, ask for several volunteers from your group to compose a panel. Have each person on the panel read a book or magazine article relating to the above-mentioned questions. Consult your church librarian or local Christian bookstore to learn what books are available. Ask each panel member to prepare a three- to five-minute report on what he has read. Inform them that a question-answer period will follow the reports.

Read James 3:1-14 each day using several translations. Study chapter 7 of the text, outlining the key points under each of the three main headings on note cards. Be prepared to summarize these ideas as suggested under *Presentation.*

Presentation

1. To introduce the third characteristic of a mature Christian, ask everyone to think of the time when they were hurt the most by someone's words. Then ask them to think of the time when they were helped the most by someone's words. Comment that words truly carry a lot of impact. We are well aware of how other's words affect us, either for harm or for good, but it is

more difficult to detect how our words are affecting others because we often say things hastily without thought, or with "righteous indignation," or defensiveness. This matter of communication and how it affects our relationships with people has been widely addressed in recent years. Many of the helpful concepts and principles set forth are rooted in truths given to us in the Book of James.

2. Introduce your guest speaker (or play taped interview, or conduct panel discussion—See *Preparation*). Allow time for the group to ask questions of the guest speaker or panel.

3. Display MTM-7, briefly summarizing the power of the tongue to direct and to destroy as the author outlines in the text. Consider in greater detail the tongue's power to delight by referring to the tree and the fountain on chalkboard 7. Ask, *What comparisons can you make between "delightful" words and a tree? What comparisons can you make between "delightful" words and a fountain?* Write responses on the chalkboard beside each sketch.

4. Draw attention once again to MTM-7. Comment that many times we talk about our tongue as though it just does what it pleases without any help from us. We say, "My tongue slipped." "I lost control of my tongue." Ask, *What is the danger in such an approach to sins of the tongue?* Have two people find and read: Matthew 12:34 and Matthew 15:18. Then read Psalm 141:3-4 from MTM-7. Stress that our words are a direct reflection of what is in our hearts—what "power cell" we are plugged into; and that is a matter of choice. Note again the comparison between delightful words and the root system of a tree. Challenge the group to be slow to speak during

Chalkboard 7
Use to consider in greater detail the tongue's power to delight.

the coming week, slow enough to consider first: *Where is my heart plugged in? What are my intentions in saying what I plan to say—to hurt or to help, to build up myself or another, to direct negatively or positively, to discourage or to delight?*

Close the session by asking each one to silently pray Psalm 141:3-4.

Anticipation

Assign the reading of James 3:13-18 in several translations and chapter 8 of the text.

Where to Get Wisdom | *Text, Chapter 8*

Session Goal

To learn to detect the difference between true and false wisdom.

Preparation

Read James 3:13-18 each day, using various translations. Study chapter 8 of the text, outlining or underlining key ideas as you read. Each day jot down on paper examples of false wisdom you find as you listen to conversations, the television or radio, or read the newspaper. Also read 1 Corinthians 1 and 2, and Proverbs 1.

Presentation

Briefly review the theme of session 7 using MTM-7. Explain how this session's theme on wisdom relates to the third characteristic of a mature Christian (see page 109 of the text). Comment that there are many people who claim to be wise, and it seems we are never short of people who are willing to give advice. But we must be careful to evaluate the advice of others, as well as our own advice to others, for James tells us that there are two kinds of wisdom: a true wisdom and a false wisdom.

In Proverbs 1, wisdom is personified as a woman shouting in the streets, warning those who neglect her counsel and choose not to fear the Lord. Ask half of the group to write a biographical sketch on true wisdom personified (Mr. True Wisdom), and the other half to write on false wisdom personified (Mr. False Wisdom). Sketches should include: *Where does he come from? What does he do for a living? How does he operate? What are some examples of his work? What is the outcome of his work?* Ask members to work individually, in pairs, or in small groups. To help clarify what is meant by "examples of his work," share some of the examples of false wisdom you jotted down during the week, or explain how false and true wisdom were working in the churches James was writing to. Tell the group that they may use hypothetical situations for that section. Allow about half of the session for this writing project and the other half for them to read their biographies to the group.

Use MTM-8 to summarize the main ideas in the text. Allow prayer partners time to pray and share with each other in closing.

Anticipation

Assign the reading of James 4:1-12 and the text, chapter 9.

How to End Wars | *Text, Chapter 9*

Session Goals
1. To understand the sources of "wars" among believers.
2. To discover the "terms of peace" that will end those wars.

Preparation
Study James 4:1-12 using various translations. Study chapter 9 of the text, noting important ideas under each heading. Read the questions given under *Presentation* and note how they correspond with the progression of ideas in the text. Write down possible responses for each question as well as what important ideas should be stressed as each question is discussed.

Clip out newspaper or magazine articles dealing with wars for use during the introduction.

Presentation
Display MTM-1 and introduce the fourth characteristic of a mature Christian. Comment that the fact of wars in the world is not new to us. Our daily newspapers report on wars between governments, wars between political parties, racial wars, business wars, and gang wars. (Hold up newspaper clippings or magazine articles reporting on various wars currently in the news.) The one place, however, that you would not expect to find wars is in the church, the body of Christ. If only that were the case!

Lead a discussion of the three kinds of wars outlined in the text by using the following questions:

1. *At war with each other. What were some of the disagreements causing Christians to war with each other in James' day? What are some of the reasons Christians war against each other today? What is the difference between the kind of judging encouraged in Matthew 7:15-20 and the kind of judging discouraged in James 4:11-12 and Matthew 7:1-5? Why are these wars a particularly sad commentary on Christianity today?* (See John 13:34-35.)

2. *At war with ourselves. According to James 4:1, what is the cause of our wars with each other? Why does the author say that the essence of sin is selfishness?* (Write on the board "selfish desires," then an arrow pointing to the words "wrong actions," and another arrow pointing to "wrong praying.") *How is it possible to "spiritually" rationalize our quarrels with other Christians? How can a Christian pray "wrong"?* (Draw attention to chalkboard 8: "The purpose of prayer is not to get man's will done in heaven, but to get God's will done on earth.")

3. *At war with God. Why do you think the author states that the first two wars are really caused by this third war—the war against God? How*

do we declare war against God? What is meant by "the world" in James 4:4? Why do you think it is often easy for the Christian to be drawn into friendship with the world? Explain the analogy between adultery and friendship with the world in James 4:4. What is meant by "the flesh"? In what sense does the Spirit of God become jealous over us in James 4:5? What is one of Satan's most potent weapons against the Christian? What is the relationship between grace and pride in James 4:6? (Draw attention to this quote from the text: "One of the problems in our churches today is that we have too many celebrities and not enough servants. Christian workers are promoted so much that there is very little place left for God's glory.") *How do the world, the flesh, and the devil act as allies when we seek to rationalize and make excuses for warring against others, ourselves, and God?*

Comment that we are all well aware of the anxieties, heartbreaks, and losses inflicted by wars—whether they are national or personal. Often, however, peace settlements are slow in coming, and the terms of peace must be negotiated and renegotiated, thus prolonging the unhappy effects of war for all involved. For the Christian however, the peace treaty has already been drawn up. We can end the pain and strife of warring with others, ourselves, and God by signing on the dotted line and adhering to the terms of settlement. (Display MTM-9 and present the terms of peace.) Close in prayer.

Chalkboard 8
Use to illustrate how a Christian can pray "wrong."

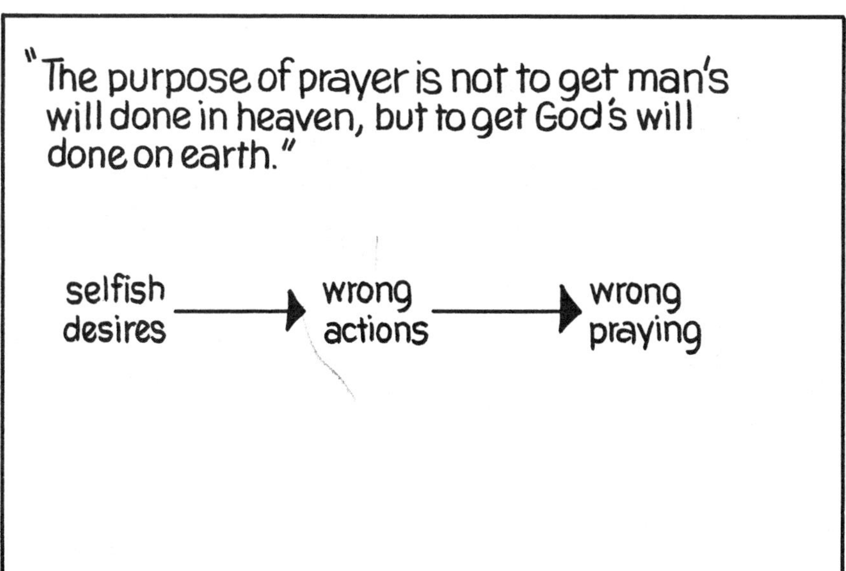

Anticipation

State: "We often hear about the will of God in very nebulous terms, and yet it is a subject that is of great importance and interest to every Christian who is serious about his walk with God. You have heard people ask, 'How can I know if this is God's will?' 'Can you ever get back into God's will once you are out of it?' We will discuss these and other issues concerning the will of God in the next session. Read James 4:13-17 several times using various translations, and read chapter 10 of the text, making special note of the reasons people give for not obeying God's will." Assign book report (see Session 10).

Plan Ahead | *Text, Chapter 10*

Session Goals

1. To have a clear understanding of what the will of God is.
2. To determine what a Christian's attitude should be toward the will of God.

Preparation

Study James 4:13-17 and chapter 10 of the text, underlining or outlining important ideas under three main headings: Ignoring God's Will; Disobeying God's Will; and Obeying God's Will.

Read the booklet, *Affirming the Will of God* by Paul E. Little published by InterVarsity Press in 1971. Ask a group member to read it also and to prepare a five-minute report for presentation at this session.

Prepare for the question-answer section of this session as you did for session 9.

Presentation

1. Briefly review the fourth characteristic of a mature Christian as discussed in the previous session, and then relate the theme of this session, the will of God, to this fourth characteristic (see pages 125-127 of the text).

2. Announce that during this session we are going to visit the "Daily Experience Train Station." Draw chalkboard 9. Ask for volunteers to participate in the following role plays (or you may wish to notify several group members in advance for a more rehearsed role play):

   a. Two Christian friends, both making their way to catch their daily trains, by chance meet at the station. Each one asks where the other one is going. Christian #1 is headed for Track 1 and Christian #2 is headed for Track 2. Christian #1 is surprised that his friend is not taking the same train and asks him why he is not. A brief discussion ensues, revealing that Christian #2 is ignoring God's will. Christian #1 tries to persuade his friend to go with him.

   b. The second situation is the same as the first except that Christian #2 reveals that he knows God's will but chooses to disobey it.

Each role play may be done more than once, according to the time you have available. Following the role plays, allow time for general comments, discussion of role play responses, and questions from the group.

Ask, *Did you notice that most of the reasons given for not following God's will were based on misconceptions of what the will of God is?*

3. State: "Let's look more specifically at what we mean by the will of God."

Display MTM-10 and ask the following questions:

How is God's will like a universal law?

Do you think that God's will for your life is detailed enough to affect your daily routine of activities? (See Ps. 37:23).

How is God's will like a living body?

What is a precondition for knowing God's will?

Do you think we can always expect to understand God's will? Why or why not?

In what respects are we always able to understand God's will? (See Text, page 137, first paragraph.)

What does it mean to "prove" God's will?

As long as we do God's will, what difference does our attitude make?

Is James advocating in 4:15 that every time we speak about our plans, we should verbally say, "If God wills"? Why or why not?

4. Ask the group if they have any questions about what has been discussed. Ask the person reporting on *Affirming the Will of God* to present his report at this time.

5. Have several people look up Mark 3:35; John 7:17; 1 John 5:14-15; and 1 John 2:15-17. Write on the chalkboard, "Benefits of Obedience" (chalkboard 9). Ask, *What are some benefits we can expect from doing the will of God?* Write responses on the chalkboard.

Close by singing (or reading the words of) "If Thou But Suffer God to Guide Thee," or another appropriate hymn.

Anticipation

State: "The next session will deal with something none of us could live without—money. As you read James 5:1-6 and chapter 11 of the text, look for basic biblical principles on how God would have us manage our money."

Chalkboard 9
Use to introduce role plays.

Money Talks | *Text, Chapter 11*

Session Goal

To consider how Christian stewardship relates to our finances.

Preparation

Study James 5:1-6 and chapter 11 of the text. List all the principles you can find in the text relating to money, and arrange them in order according to the outline shown on chalkboard 10. For your own enrichment, try to expand this list of principles by studying other Scripture passages relating to these same issues. A concordance or topical Bible will be a good study aid for this purpose. Be prepared to give examples to the group as you explain the Money Manual activity, and to give help to any subgroups that may need assistance. You may also want to share with the group any principles you found from your own study which supplement the group's findings. Prepare and gather teaching aids and materials.

Presentation

1. Display MTM-1 to review the topic of the previous session and to introduce the fifth characteristic of the mature Christian. Comment that in many respects, times have not changed much since James' day; even then people talked about national economy, business deals, and getting rich. And, as today, some people possessed an overabundance of wealth and others did not have enough to get by. Ask, *From your reading, what would you say were some of the unethical practices common among many of the wealthy of James' day?* Say, "It's easy for us to point the finger at those people who so flagrantly abused their wealth, causing misery for many less fortunate than they. But even in such extreme examples as these, there is a lesson for us—the lesson of stewardship." Ask, *What does the term "stewardship" mean?* Stress that all the money God gives us is His. We are allowed to possess it, but God still owns it and we will be held accountable for how we use it. That is why it is important to evaluate all aspects of our money management, not merely the matter of how much we give to the church every year.

2. Tell the group that they will be compiling a "Christians' Money Manual" based on their reading in James and in the text, and on any other Scriptures they can find relevant to principles of money management. Divide the group into three sections. Assign to each section the topics under one of the Roman numerals on chalkboard 10. Ask that each topic be discussed and that biblical principles be formulated pertaining to each topic. Scripture references should be given for each principle stated. Make a concordance or topical Bible available to each group.

When the groups have finished, ask a spokesman from each group to present their portion of the manual, reading both the principles and the Scripture verses supporting them. Encourage feedback from the other groups following each presentation.

3. After the presentations, collect the worksheets of each group so that you may compile The Christians' Money Manual from their work and give everyone a copy of it at the next session.

Close the session in prayer.

Anticipation

State: "One of the most common questions asked by non-Christians, and perhaps even Christians, is: *Why does God allow suffering in the world?* While part of the answer to this question is unknown to us and we must temporarily suspend judgment (as we learned in Session 3, from the book *In Two Minds*), we are still able to know some parts of the answer. As you read chapter 12 in the text, underline the reasons you find why God allows suffering in the Christian's life."

Chalkboard 10
Use for discussion on money.

A Christian and His Money

I. Obtaining Money
1. Being a good employer
2. Being a good employee

II. Using Money
1. Paying bills and taxes
2. Possessions
3. Savings and investments
4. Giving to the needy
5. Giving to God

III. Futures in Money
1. Returns on proper use
2. Returns on abuse

The Power of Patience / *Text, Chapter 12*

Session Goal

To be encouraged to be patient when enduring physical troubles, knowing that: (1) When Christ returns, there will be an end to suffering; and (2) until that time, there is always a purpose in the Christian's suffering.

Preparation

Prepare copies of The Christians' Money Manual for each group member (see Session 11).

Study James 5:7-12 in several translations and chapter 12 of the text. Familiarize yourself with the passages in Job that are referred to in the *Presentation*. Anticipate possible answers to questions given in the *Presentation,* particularly the Neighbor Nudging discussion questions.

Prepare and gather materials needed.

Presentation

Distribute copies of The Christians' Money Manual you prepared from the previous session's activity, commenting positively on the group's work. Say, "You recall that many of the people James was writing to were experiencing grave economic troubles because of the oppression of the rich. Many that James addressed were also experiencing physical troubles and James sought to encourage them in the text we are exploring today. James had warned the rich oppressors that they would not escape judgment. He continued by saying, 'Be patient, *therefore,* brethren' (5:7, emphasis added). Just as the tyranny of the rich would surely end, so there would surely be an end to their suffering. When Christ returns, there will be no more injustice, persecution, disease or death. The people reading James' letter must have sighed, 'What a blessed day; oh, that He would come soon!' But James did not end his encouragement on that note. There was one other reason to be patient in suffering, and he gave them three examples to illustrate his point."

1. *The Farmer.* Display MTM-11 and ask, *Why does a farmer have to be patient? How are we like "spiritual farmers"? What do the soil, seed, seasons, and harvest typify?* Discuss each of the instructions to the "spiritual farmer" as follows:

    a. "Be Patient." Ask, *What is the spiritual farmer to be patient for?*

    b. "Establish Your Heart." Ask, *What does it mean to establish your heart?* Have several members with different Bible translations read 5:8 to compare renderings of this word. Ask, *Why does the author say, "You can enjoy this kind of harvest* (the harvest the farmer is patient for, above) *only if your heart is established*"? *What are some concrete things we can do to establish our hearts?*

c. "Keep Working." Ask, *As we wait for the Lord's return, what should we be working on?*

d. "Don't Use Your Sickle on Your Neighbors." Ask, *Why is this kind of behavior self-defeating?*

2. *The Prophets.* Have each member skim over pages 156-158 of the text and "Nudge his Neighbor" (see front material in this *Guide*) on the question: *In what ways are we encouraged by the examples of the prophets who suffered?* After five to seven minutes, ask for their responses to the question. Write ideas on the chalkboard.

3. *Job.* Ask someone familiar with Job to summarize the events of his life. Have each person skim over Job 31; 38; 40:1-9 and 42:1-6. Then with the same neighbor each one had for the previous question, have the groups discuss the question: *What do you think caused the difference in Job's attitude between his discourse in chapter 31 and his response to God in chapter 42?* Conduct group discussion as before.

Comment that Job may have caught a glimpse of this concept. No Christian suffers without reason, though that reason may be beyond his human understanding. Job said, "I know that Thou canst do all things, and that *no purpose of Thine can be thwarted* . . . I have declared that which I did not understand, things too wonderful for me, which I did not know" (Job 42:2-3, NASB, emphasis added). *Why can we be patient in suffering?* (Because it's part of God's careful plan for us; it's no mistake.)

Comment that though many times we don't know the *specific* reason for suffering in our lives, God has revealed to us through His Word some of the things He accomplishes in Christians through suffering. Ask, *What are some of them?* Write responses on chalkboard 11 (produces fruit, builds character, prepares us for greater blessing, reveals Himself in some new way, keeps us humble, makes us a testimony to others).

Close in prayer, thanking God that He has chosen to fit us into His marvelous plans and produce a harvest in our lives that is worth being patient for.

<table>
<tr><td>

What does God accomplish in Christians through SUFFERING?

1. Fruit
2. Character
3. Preparation for greater blessing
4. Revelation of Himself in some new way
5. Humility
6. Testimony

</td><td>

Chalkboard 11
Use to show what God can accomplish in a Christian's life through suffering.

</td></tr>
</table>

Anticipation

Say, "Many new books on the market today are on the subject of prayer. It seems that many people are discovering, or rediscovering, that great things can be accomplishd through prayer. As you read chapter 13 in the text for the next session, you will find out what some of these great things are."

Let Us Pray / *Text, Chapter 13*

Session Goal

To realize the value of prayer in coping with the troubles of life.

Preparation

Study James 5:13-20 in several translations and chapter 13 of the text, underlining or outlining key ideas as you read. Anticipate responses to the suggested discussion questions and be prepared to add any important ideas which the group may leave out.

Skim through some of the recently published books on prayer that you have available to you, and look for helpful suggestions for establishing and maintaining an effective prayer life (allotting time, lists and diaries, partners and conversational prayer, keeping your mind on track, etc.). When all contributions from the group have been given for the "Helps" column of MTM-12, add any others you found from your research.

Prepare and gather teaching aids and materials.

Presentation

Say, "During the last session we discussed some of the reasons God permits suffering in our lives; God is producing a harvest in us and He has chosen us to be part of His marvelous eternal plans. While knowledge of these facts surely helps us to be patient in the midst of suffering, there is also something we can actively *do* to cope with suffering. *Can you guess what that is?"* Ask, *What concrete results can be accomplished through the prayers of, and for, the suffering believer?*

James specifically mentions three other "trouble areas" where prayer "availeth much." Divide the group into three subgroups for discussion of these three areas. Assign one topic with corresponding questions to each group. Write the questions on note cards or on a blank transparency.

1. *Prayer for the Sick.* *What were the specific circumstances surrounding the prayer offered for the sick in James 5:14-16?*

What is "the prayer of faith"?

What are some practical lessons we can learn from these verses?

What part should modern medicine have in healing our illness? Why?

What damage can be done if sin is confessed beyond the circle of its influence?

2. *Prayer for the Nation.* It is easy to wonder what good one ordinary person's prayer for a large nation like ours would do. *What factors from the story of Elijah would indicate to the contrary?*

Why is it impossible to "separate the Word of God and prayer"?

What is the difference between the "much praying" mentioned in Matthew 6:7, and being persistent in prayer?

What do you think the author meant when he said, "Many people do not pray in their prayers"?

3. *Prayer for the Straying.* *What does it mean to "backslide"?*

What part does love play in helping a straying fellow Christian?

In many Christian churches today, confronting a Christian brother about his sin is the last thing to be done, if it is done at all. Why do you think this is the case?

While the reference in 5:19-20 is primarily to the straying believer, what application do these same verses have to a nonbeliever?

After 10 to 15 minutes, have the groups reassemble and present the results of their discussions. One person from each group may answer all the questions, or different people may be responsible for answering one question.

Display MTM-12 and comment that while God plainly tells us how valuable prayer is in our Christian life, it often seems like a most difficult thing to do. Ask, *What are some of the problems or frustrations you encounter when trying to establish and maintain a regular prayer time?* Write responses under "Hindrances" on MTM-12. Ask, *What are some practical helps you have discovered to overcome these prayer hindrances?* Write responses under "Helps."

Display MTM-1 and comment that we have come to the end of our study on the Book of James. Ask that everyone turn to the back of the text to review once more the questions dealing with our own spiritual maturity. As you read each question aloud, draw attention to the characteristic of the mature Christian on the MTM to which the question relates.

Allow extra time for the closing of the session, asking that prayer partners share and pray for each other that they may be able to practice the truths they have learned in this study.